# BEWARE AMERICA

## A Message to the President

by
Dr. Charles R. Taylor

*Published by*
Today in Bible Prophecy, Inc.
P.O. Box 5700
Huntington Beach, CA 92615

ISBN 0-937682-06-3
© 1983, Today in Bible Prophecy, Inc.
All rights reserved.

## INTRODUCTION

This booklet is the manuscript of a special message sent to President Ronald Reagan, his Cabinet members and the Congress. The reason for the message is in the title: BEWARE AMERICA!

News events today fit the pattern of specific prophecies written in the Bible centuries ago. This nation, the United States of America, is described in detail and its destiny is proclaimed. Although it is not called by name, it is the only nation on Earth that fits the description in the prophecy. Even the recorded vision of Gen. George Washington at Valley Forge, mentioned in this message, fits the prophecy.

From the time of the assassination of Egyptian President Anwar Sadat, the Arabs have pressed for a Palestinian state and war with Israel. When the U.S. and Western European powers defend Israel from the combined Soviet and Arab armies, World War III will happen.

The New Age Movement will be dominant in religion. Beware of the so-called Guardian Angels. This message tells why.

America's judgement is coming, but it will live through it. Note my recommendations for survival and victory.

The message will speak for itself—and be a blessing to you.

Dr. Charles R. Taylor

# BEWARE AMERICA

*Manuscript of the cassette message sent
by Dr. Charles R. Taylor in November, 1982,
to President Ronald Reagan*

---

This is a special message to the President of the United States of America, to the Vice President, the Cabinet and the Congress. It is a message of information relative to the well being of the people of this great nation.

We face a crisis of very serious magnitude, including a probable attack by the USSR, the Soviet Union. Bible prophecy portrays it and almost every newspaper has information concerning the preparations for it.

I have documented this type of detail for more than 40 years. I have spoken in hundreds of churches and colleges, have had a radio program since 1965 and have produced the television program TODAY IN BIBLE PROPHECY since 1974, broadcasting coast-to-coast. My name is Dr. Charles R. Taylor. I am founder and president of Today in Bible Prophecy, Inc. of Anaheim, California.

## TRENDS TOWARD WORLD WAR III

Every president of the United States since Harry S. Truman has proclaimed the solidarity of the U.S.A. with the nation of Israel. This is biblical and proper. It also can be dangerous. The U.S. is not headed for Armageddon, but it shall see a dreadful war. Ask the Defense Department, the OCD or AEC. It no longer is a question of "whether"—only "WHEN?"

In this message, I shall convey from specific Bible prophecies the exact nations that are to be involved and what the results of the conflict will be. Listen carefully, for the time is almost at hand.

## Beware America

President Anwar Sadat of Egypt was shot to death while watching a military parade, October 6, 1981. As documented on page 53 of my recent book, *DEATH OF SADAT...START OF WORLD WAR III*, Libyan leader Col. Moammar Khadafy congratulated the assassins of President Anwar Sadat and called on the Egyptian Army to oust other officials of the pro-Western government.

On October 13, 1981, Associated Press reported from Damascus, Syria, that "Syria's government-controlled media hailed the 'execution' of the Egyptian President and warned that other Egyptian leaders face 'the same fate as the traitor' if they continue his policies."

Investigations in Cairo proved that five Moslem fundamentalist groups had joined ranks to plot Sadat's assassination. More than 6,000 such Moslems were arrested within the month to ensure greater security.

International Moslem attitudes were evident when only three of the 18 Arab states sent representatives to Sadat's funeral. There was to be no association with any person or government that had contact with Israel.

Little tolerance was shown. However, shortly after the funeral a veteran Mideast observer in Beirut said, "If the new rulers of Egypt stick to the Camp David accord for the time being in order to secure the return of the Sinai from the Israelis, there will be understanding from other Arab nations." He added, "It is only afterwards that Egypt will be expected to resume its rightful position in the mainstream of the Arab world."

The last of the Sinai was returned to Egypt on April 25, 1982.

July 6, 1982, Associated Press, CAIRO: "President Hosni Mubarak accepted an invitation Monday to attend a non-aligned summit in Iraq—an important step toward reconciliation with the Arab world. The invitation to visit the capital of one of the Arab world's most radical and anti-Israel countries was the latest development in the slow process of restoring links shattered by President Anwar Sadat's visit to Israel in 1977.

An article in August 2, 1982, U.S. News and World Report states that Egypt's President Hosni Mubarak has moved to "front-runner in the leadership of the Arab world," unquote.

## RELATED BIBLE PROPHECIES

Bible prophecy does reveal that Egypt will lead the Arab nations in another attack against Israel and that Egypt, its allies and its helpers will suffer a tremendous defeat. Isaiah 19:17 says, "The land of Judah shall be a terror unto Egypt, everyone that makes mention thereof shall be afraid in himself." Ezekiel 39:4 says, "Thou shalt fall on the mountains of Israel."

Ezekial 38, which lists most of the nations to be involved in this great war that we commonly call World War III, lists the Arab world under the terms "Persia, Ethiopia and Libya." Libya refers to the Arab region west of Egypt; Ethiopia means the Arab and Ethiopian region south of Egypt. Egypt, itself, is included under the term Persia, because Persia conquered Egypt right after the time of Ezekiel—in 525 B.C.—and controlled it for almost 200 years. Persia (the Iran of today) ruled over the entire Middle East from Egypt to Turkey to Pakistan from 525 B.C. until conquered by Alexander the Great in 323 B.C.

The prophet Daniel also foretold the coming defeat of Egypt and its allies by stating in Daniel 11:42 and 43, "The land of Egypt shall not escape. But he (the Antichrist king of the Tribulation Period) shall have power over the treasures of gold and silver, and over all the precious things of Egypt; and the Libyans and Ethiopians shall be at his steps." Just as Ezekiel listed, "PERSIA, ETHIOPIA AND LIBYA," the prophet Daniel listed EGYPT and the LIBYANS and the ETHIOPIANS. All three of these prophets—Isaiah, Ezekial and Daniel—declared that this triumvirate of Arab states would be defeated, Isaiah including the Soviet-Warsaw Pact nations as, quote, "they that are the stay of the tribes thereof (of Egypt and the Arab states).

Ezekiel was even more specific, naming the regions of the U.S.S.R. and the Warsaw Pact as well as "PERSIA, ETHIOPIA AND LIBYA." He proclaimed God's declaration against the Soviets in Ezekiel 38:1-3. Listen as I read it; "And the word of the Lord came unto me saying, Son of man, set your face against Gog, the land of Magog, the chief prince of Meshech and Tubal, and prophesy against him, and say, Thus saith the Lord God: Behold, I am against thee, O Gog, the chief prince of Meshech and Tubal."

By definition, these names are clarified by the first book of the Bible, in Geneisis 10. Magog, Meshech and Tubal were grandsons of Noah, sons of Japheth, who settled in the Soviet area. Magog dwelt in southern Russia, Meshech in central and northern Russia (Moscow was named after Meshech) and Tubal settled in Siberia. Tobolsk, the former capital of Siberia was named after Tubal.

The remarkable thing about this, is that God was prophesying through Ezekiel that in the latter years there would be one prince over them all. This was fulfilled in 1923 when the Treaty of Union was signed that united Russia and Siberia. Thus was formed the U.S.S.R., the Union of Soviet Socialist Republics, with its one capital and one leader in the Kremlin. Being an atheistic nation, it is against God; and, therefore, God declares in Ezekiel 38:3, "I am against thee, O Gog, THE CHIEF PRINCE of Meshech and Tubal."

In Ezekiel 38:5, Persia (including Egypt), plus Ethiopia and Libya are listed as being "with" the Soviets.

Gomer and "Togarmah of the north quarters" are listed in the next verse. Gomer was another brother of Magog, Meshech and Tubal. He settled in eastern Europe—Germany being named after him. His son, Togarmah's family, settled two areas: Turkey in the south and the Baltic states of Latvia, Lithuania and Estonia in the north. The term "Togarmah of the north quarters" relates to the Baltic states now already absorbed by and contolled by the Soviet Union.

It is thus that we see that all of Eastern Europe (Warsaw Pact nations) and all of the U.S.S.R. plus all the Arab states are listed in Ezekiel 38 as being in alliance: as being together. Verse 8 reads, "After many days: in the latter years thou shalt come into the land that is brought back from the sword, and is gathered out of many people, against the mountains of Israel." Ezekiel even saw air power, for he stated in verse 9, "Thou shalt come like a storm, thou shalt be like a cloud to cover the land, thou and all thine armies, and many people with thee." THESE ARE THE NATIONS THAT WILL OPPOSE ISRAEL IN THE COMING WAR.

## THE DEFENDERS OF ISRAEL

For a list of the nations that will defend Israel in the coming war, we have to go to other portions of the Bible. According to Bible prophecy, Egypt, representing the Arab states, will be defeated by a military king. Daniel 11:42 states, "He shall stretch forth his hand upon the countries: and the land of Egypt shall not escape." The military leader referred to is described a few verses earlier, in Daniel 11:36. It reads, "And THE KING shall do according to his will; and he shall exalt himself, and magnify himself above every god, and shall speak marvellous things against the God of gods, and shall prosper till the indignation be accomplished: for that that is determined shall be done." This is a prophecy that shall surely come to pass, and THE KING referred to is to be the Antichrist of "the time of the end"—the Tribulation Period.

It is part of God's eternal plan of the ages that there shall be an end-time fierce ruler called "THE KING," "the prince who shall come," "THE BEAST" of the books of Daniel and Revelation. Since he will be contrary to the Christians, he commonly is referred to as THE ANTICHRIST. He will be a king and a military ruler. In Daniel 7, he is referred to as being the king who will be the military leader of the eleventh nation to join the 10-nation portion of the revived Roman empire, recognized by virtually all students of eschatology as being the European Community, the Common Market of today.

Let me verify this for you. Daniel, chapter 7, describes the great Gentile empires that ruled over the land of Israel. Using animals as illustrations, verse 4 describes Babylon as being "like a lion." Verse 5 describes the Medo-Persian empire as being "like to a bear." The Greek empire is referred to as being "like a leopard" and the strong Roman empire as being a "dreadul and terrible beast—and it had ten horns." For seven centuries—264 B.C. to A.D. 476—the Romans ruled over many nations. However, there never was a 10-nation entity in that era. That only became a reality when Greece joined the Common Market January 1, 1981. The Revived Roman Empire first became evident with the signing of the Treaty of Rome on March 25, 1957. Six nations joined together to form the European Economic Community. They were Luxembourg, Belgium, The Netherlands, Italy, France and West Germany. Britain, Ireland and Denmark joined January 1, 1973 and Greece became the tenth member January 1, 1981.

Now note the prophecy of Daniel 7, verses 8 and 24, wherein the Revived Roman Empire is described as having an eleventh member and a notable KING. Following the statement about the ten horns in verse 7, it reads, "I considered the horns, and, behold, there came up among them another little horn, before whom there were three of the first horns plucked up by the roots: and, behold, in this horn were the eyes of a man, and a mouth speaking great things." Verse 24 enlarges on the description: "The ten horns out of this kingdom are ten kings that shall arise: and *another* shall rise *after them;* and *he shall be different from the first,* and he shall subdue three kings. And he shall speak great words against the most High, and shall wear out the saints of the most High, and think to change times and laws." THIS ONE IS TO BECOME A POWERFUL KING—THE ANTICHRIST.

## MORE DETAIL CONCERNING THE ANTICHRIST KING

Concerning the end-time king, a similar description of him is recorded in Revelation 17, verses 12 and 13: "And the ten horns which you saw are ten kings, which have recieved no kingdom as yet; but receive power as kings one hour with the beast. These shall have one mind, and shall give their power and strength unto the beast."

The established ten kings (leaders) of the revived Roman entity will all agree to place one man, a king, in authority. He is to be THE KING of the end-time, and he will be the king of the next nation to join the European Community, for he is to be *different from the first ten members.*

There is strong evidence today that Spain will become the eleventh nation to join the European Community. Spain became a member of NATO May 30, 1982, a prerequisite to become a member of the Common Market. It also has signed most of the agreements relative to the Economic Community, only fishing and agriculture remaining to be negotiated. When these are complete—soon—Spain will be ready to sign the Treaty of Accession which will establish it as the next nation to join the European Community. Its leader, King Juan Carlos I,

COULD, therefore become the prophesied one who will lead in the defense of Israel, protecting Israel from the Soviet and Arab attack.

In Daniel 9:26, THE KING who is to do this is referred to as "the prince who shall come." Part of Daniel 9:26 reads: "And the people of the prince who shall come shall destroy the city and the sanctuary." Jerusalem and its sanctuary, the Temple, were destroyed in A.D. 70 by the Roman legions. It is interesting to not that King Juan Carlos I was *born in Rome* January 5, 1938. From this standpoint, he fulfills the qualification. Daniel 9:27 states that this same leader will make a covenant to protect Israel for a period of seven years. Whoever is king at that time will be the one to protect Israel when the time comes. Further verification of this is found in Daniel, chapter 11. Verse 36 describes the king who "shall exalt himself." Verse 37 says he will "magnify himself above all." Verses 38 and 39 say he will "honor the god of forces" and costly munitions. Yes, he is to be a strong military man—not a man of peace as some people imply. That concept comes from the fact that he will guarantee Israel's peace and security for seven years. But that pseudo-peace will only come after World War III. How do we know? Look at the scenario given in the Bible.

## BIBLE SCENARIO OF THINGS TO COME

By the time the war comes, this Antichrist king will have been given full authority by the leaders of the Common Market countries and will have signed the treaty with Israel. This is verified by the terminology of Daniel 11:40.

We know from the prophecies in Ezekiel 38 and 39 that the Arabs and the Soviets will attack the nation of Israel. But in Daniel 11:40 it is written, "At the time of the end shall the king of the south (the Arab nations) push *at him.*" That is, at the

Antichrist king. It is so stated because the military power of the Western European nations already will be under the control of the Antichrist, and this king already will have committed that mighty power to Israel's protection. In other words, the guarantee already will be in force.

Notice also that the last half of Daniel 11:40 states, "and the king of the north (leader of the Soviet forces) will come *against him* like a whirlwind with armaments and with many ships." (The Soviet Union today has the largest navy in the world.) "And he (this end-time king) will enter into the countries (those that oppose Israel), and shall overflow...He shall enter also into the glorious land (Israel), and many countries shall be overthrown." Yes, this military leader will claim many victories and take over many countries. He will take the honor for the defeat of the Soviet and Arab armies, regardless of the manner in which it is accomplished.

BUT WILL HE DO IT ALONE? NOT AT ALL, FOR THE NUCLEAR ARSENAL OF THE U.S.A. WILL BE GREATLY INVOLVED.

The early portion of Ezekiel 38 gives you the line-up of the nations that are to attack Israel. Then, verse 15 begins to describe the war: "And thou shalt come from they place out of the north parts (Moscow is straight north of Jerusalem), thou, and many people (the Warsaw Pact nations) with thee, a great company and a mighty army: and thou shalt come up *against my people of Israel,* as a cloud to cover the land; *and it shall be in the latter days."* Verse 18 reads, "And it shall come to pass at the same time when Gog (leader of the Soviet military forces) shall come against the land of Israel, saith the Lord God, that my fury will come up in my face." Verse 21 says, *"And I will call for a sword against him* throughout all my mountains, saith the Lord God." Ezekiel 39:4 states, *"Thou shalt fall* upon the mountains of Israel, thou, and all thine armies, and the people that is with thee: I will give thee to the ravenous birds...Thou shalt fall on the open field for I have spoken it, saith the Lord God."

The Soviet and Arab armies will be horribly defeated on the mountains of Israel. I have documentations in my files that Israel has extremely potent nerve gas, has neutron weapons and also atomic bombs. Israel, itself, has an arsenal that can halt a mighty army. But Israel also will have the help of the nations of Western Europe and of the mighty NATO ally thereof, the United States of America. Yes, the U.S.A. will be greatly involved.

Ezekiel 39:6 proclaims, "And I will send a fire on Magog (Russia) and among them that dwell carelessly in the isles (the coastland of Western Europe and the U.S.A.)." There is going to be a heavy nuclear exchange, but not on Israel. The nuclear battle primarily will be against the Soviet Union and, also, Russia's nuclear power will be unleashed against the cities of Western Europe and against our land, the United States of America.

CAN IT BE? Pick up any newspaper for verification. But a more sure way is to look into the inspired word of God, the Bible. Note the words of the great Hebrew prophet, Isaiah, reading from Isaiah 13:4-14, "The noise of a multitude in the mountains, like as of a great people: a tumultuous noise of the kingdoms of nations gathered together: The Lord of hosts mustereth the host of the battle.

*"They come from a far country,* from the end of heaven, even the *weapons of His indignation,* to destroy the whole land...And they shall be afraid: they shall be amazed one at another; *their faces shall be as flames.*

"Behold, the day of the Lord cometh, cruel both with wrath and fierce anger, to lay the land desolate...And I will punish the world for their evil, and the wicked for their iniquity: and I will cause the arrogancy of the proud to cease, and will lay low the haughtiness of the terrible."

Isaiah 24 reads, "...the haughty people of the earth do languish. The earth also is defiled under the inhabitants thereof; because they have transgressed the laws, changed the ordinance, broken the everlasting covenant. THEREFORE hath the curse devoured the earth, and they that dwell therein are desolate: THEREFORE, *the inhabitants of the earth are burned,* and few men left."

Listen to the prophet Joel, who wrote about 800 years before Jesus ever walked on earth. In Joel 2 it is written, "A great people and a strong: there hath not been ever the like, neither shall be any more after it, even to the years of many generations." (Devastation will be so great. Other Bible prophecies declare that one-fourth of the people of earth will die in a one-day nuclear battle by fire.) Verse 3 reads, "A FIRE devoureth before them; and behind them A FLAME burneth: the land is as the garden of Eden before them, and behind them a desolate wilderness; yea, and nothing shall escape them...*a strong people set in battle array*...the people shall be much pained: all faces shall gather blackness."

WHAT A PICTURE! A perfect description of atomic warfare: "As a garden of Eden before them, and behind them a desolate wilderness." In the book of Revelation, chapter 8, we find that one-third of the earth will be burned, one-third of all trees destroyed and all green grass burnt up. We find also that one-third of the ships of the sea will be destroyed and the people in them die. God knew that in this atomic age, much of the nuclear power would be in the ships and the submarines. Our Trident submarines now are being launched, but the Soviet Union has a sizable fleet of their Typhoon Class submarines that are larger than any submarine we have ever built. Theirs are so large they can be stationed in the South

Pacific and still hit any city in the United States with their 6,000-mile missiles. Or they can be at home base in Murmansk on the Arctic Circle, shoot over the North Pole and hit any or all of the cities of America.

In addition, a report from Washington dated April 6, 1982, states that the Soviet Union has deployed almost 200 mobile intercontinental ballistic missiles (ICBMs). While we argue about what to do with the MX missiles, the Soviets have been building theirs and placing them in position. This article states, quote, "Now, evidence of actual deployment of the world's first mobile ICMB is incontrovertible. The dread 6,000-nautical-mile missiles, housed in and fired from huge, wheeled vehicles capable of rapid movement, are concealed under elaborate camouflage in the Plesetsk region."

But they are not alone. New York Times reported on March 22, 1982, that President Reagan has endorsed a plan that calls for production over the next five years of about 380 more nuclear warheads than the number planned by the Carter Administration. It is believed that the current American stockpile of nuclear weapons totals about 25,000. Both U.S. and the Soviets have enough nuclear weapons to make a cinder out of either nation, and the destruction of cities of 50,000 or more population is still the paramount plan, plus the many aimed at strategic arms targets.

Remember that God's Word says the He will "call for a sword" (warfare) against the land of the Soviets and that He would "send a fire on the land of Magog." Before me is an Associated Press report of February 17, 1982, which states, "The Strategic Air Command developed a battle plan in the 1950s to reduce the Soviet Union to a 'smoking, radiating ruin' in two hours, according to recently declassified material. The SAC plan called for 735 bombers to overwhelm Soviet defenses and drop 600 to 750 nuclear bombs. Chief targets would be airfieleds and atomic installations, but military planners estimated 118 major cities would be destroyed and 60 million people killed." And that was in the 1950s: think of what we can do today!

In this message, I am presenting only a few of the many known facts concerning preparations for the coming war. I am not advocating such a war, but am emphasizing the fact that *it is prophesied in the Bible*, and it is about to happen!

## DECLARATIONS ABOUT THE UNITED STATES

Entirely apart from the Bible, there is another prophecy worthy of consideration. It fits the Bible pattern but is totally independent from it. I speak of the vision seen by Gen. George Washington at Valley Forge in the winter of 1777. By a visiting angel, he was shown the birth, progress and the destiny of the United States of America. That vision account is too long to quote in its fullness, but you can read it in my major book *WORLD WAR III AND THE DESTINY OF AMERICA*.

For our purpose, here is the summary: General Washington was shown by a vision that this country would endure three great wars: the Revolutionary War then in progress, the Civil War within one hundred years and a third, fearful, war. Here is a portion of his account related to World War III:

"The dark, shadowy angel placed a trumpet to his mouth and blew three distinct blasts; and taking from the ocean, he sprinkled it upon Europe, Asia and Africa. Then my eyes beheld a fearful scene. From each of these continents arose thick black clouds that were soon joined into one. And through this mass there gleamed a dark red light by which I saw hordes of armed men. These men, moving with the cloud, marched by land and sailed by sea to America, which country was enveloped in the volume of the cloud. And I saw these vast armies devastate the whole country and burn the villages, towns and cities which I had seen springing up.

"As my ears listened to the thundering of the cannon, clashing of swords, and the shouts and cries of millions in mortal combat, I again heard the mysterious voice saying, 'SON OF THE REPUBLIC, LOOK AND LEARN'... Instantly a light as of a thousand suns shone down from above me, and broke into fragments the dark cloud which enveloped America. At the same moment the angel upon whose head still shone the word 'UNION,' and who bore our national flag in one hand and a sword in the other, descended from the heavens attended by legions of white spirits. These immediately joined the inhabitants of America, who I perceived were well-nigh overcome, but who immediately taking courage again, closed up their ranks and renewed the battle, leaving the inhabitants of the land victorious.

"Then once more, I beheld the villages, towns and cities springing up where I had seen them before, while the bright angel, planting the azure standard he had brought in the midst of them, cried with a loud voice: 'WHILE THE STARS REMAIN, AND THE HEAVENS SEND DOWN DEW UPON THE EARTH, SO LONG WILL THE UNION LAST.'

"This also disappeared, and I found myself once more gazing upon the mysterious visitor, who, in the same voice I had heard before, said, 'SON OF THE REPUBLIC, WHAT YOU HAVE SEEN IS THUS INTERPRETED. THREE GREAT PERILS WILL COME UPON THE REPUBLIC. THE MOST FEARFUL FOR HER IS THE THIRD. BUT THE WHOLE WORLD UNITED SHALL NOT PREVAIL AGAINST HER. LET EVERY CHILD OF THE REPUBLIC LEARN TO LIVE FOR HIS GOD, HIS LAND AND UNION.'"

This vision of Gen. George Washington, seen over 200 years ago, shows a prophetic picture of the United States being in a fearful war with nations from three continents. PERSIA, ETHIOPIA AND THE SOVIET UNION WITH ITS WARSAW PACT ARMIES WOULD BE, PRECISELY, FROM THE THREE CONTINENTS MENTIONED—ASIA, AFRICA AND EUROPE. The cities of America are portrayed as being in flames, indicating a nuclear exchange. But I am happy to point out that Gen. George Washington also saw these villages, towns and cities being rebuilt. He saw victory!

## MY PERSONAL OBSERVATIONS

More than that, Mr. President, I can show you from the Scripture that God's Word, THE BIBLE, portrays that the United States of America will endure its trial and will continue as a nation, bringing its present year by year to the place where the Lord of hosts eventually will reign as King over all the earth.

I do not speak lightly, for I have studied the prophecies of the Bible—from cover to cover—for more than 50 years. The prophecies coordinate into a great panorama of the Ages, and I have good news for you: in the long run, WE WIN!

But this haughty and proud nation with its heavy crime and gross immorality has corrupted itself and is ripe for judgment.

This "careless" land is mentioned several times in the Bible, but one special chapter refers to, and can *only* refer to, the United States of America. Our destiny is described in the 18th chapter of Isaiah. Heavy documentations and proofs of this are provided in my 390-page book *WORLD WAR III AND THE DESTINY OF AMERICA*. The heart of the message, however, is in just four verses of that chapter. Isaiah 18:4 reads, "And the Lord said unto me, I will take my rest, and I will consider in my dwelling place (God says He is going to sit down and take a look at this nation), and it will be like a clear heat upon herbs or a cloud of dew in the heat of harvest." That is not a good omen, for clear heat wilts herbs or a cloud of dew at time of harvest will cause mildew and great loss of the grain. It is a symbol of judgment. In that coming judgment, He likens this nation to a grape vine, and then makes some specific declarations.

Someone, He says, an enemy, is going to "cut off the sprigs with pruning hooks, and take away and cut down the branches" of this nation. Only one country on earth would dare to attack the United States, and that nation is Russia, or, more properly, the Soviet Union. Its goal since its inception has been to destroy capitalism and its chief proponent, the U.S.A. And the Soviet Union has backed the PLO and the Arab states in every way in their fight against Israel, faltering only in the case of the PLO in Lebanon where it was considered to be a lost cause.

The Soviet Union is very much aware of the deep U.S. commitment to protect Israel. The leaders of the Kremlin *know* that any time they attack Israel they will have to deal with the U.S. and with Western Europe. When the eleventh king takes over, though, the stand of Western Europe will be even stronger. THAT TIME IS VERY NEAR.

But let's get back to the Isaiah 18 prophecy about our own land, the United States of America. At what point in time will this Soviet attack occur? Will there be another great depression and will we see "the death of the dollar" as some are indicating? My answer is an absolute "NO!"

Listen carefully to the message of Isaiah 18, verse 5: "For *before* the harvest, when the bud is perfect, and the sour grape is ripening in the flower" (In other words, when this nation is at the very peak of its strength—as when the grapes are ripening just before the harvest: that is when the judgment will come), "He," an outside force and enemy, "shall both cut off the sprigs with pruning hooks, and take away and cut down the branches." My friends, I see it as being at a time when the U.S.

is affluent and in the height of its monetary and productive strength that it will be attacked and "pruned" and "cut." According to that description, it could happen at any moment!

Remember, however, that the vine will not be destroyed. Many of the "branches," referring to our cities, will be "cut down" in this attack, for it will be a furious one in which our great cities will be in flames all across the country. It will be a severe war. The nuclear fury will only last one day, but the anarchy and disruptions as well as very possible overseas attacks will continue for most of the seven years of the Tribulation Period.

The next verse of Isaiah 18, however, is reassuring, for it states: "They shall be left together unto the fowls of the mountains, and to the beasts of the earth." America will be greatly damaged, but it will survive. It will not be destroyed.

The last verse reads: "In that time (after the conflict is over) shall the present be brought unto the Lord of hosts (referring to the Messiah-Deliverer who will bring Peace on Earth after the seven years of Satanic oppression and tribulation). The U.S.A. will bring its present to the Lord in appreciation of His deliverance, and it is described as coming from "A PEOPLE" (such as the preamble to the Constitution says, "We, THE PEOPLE OF THE UNITED STATES, in order to form a more perfect Union"). The U.S. is "scattered and peeled" or, more properly translated, "outspread and polished"—a highly developed nation having the highest standard of living in the world. "From a people tenacious from their beginning hitherto"—from a nation that has never lost a war and had as one of its early flags the Rattlesnake Flag with its inscription "DON'T TREAD ON ME!" "A nation measured out and trodden down"—and no nation on earth is so extensively measured and traversed, our nation consisting of a 50-state land area of 3,615,211 square miles traversed by 3,838,146 lineal miles of roadways plus 199,215 miles of railroad tracks as of December 31, 1975. Most assuredly it can be said that this land is traversed and "trodden down." And finally, a country whose land "the rivers have spoiled." Perhaps it could be said they are spoiled from an ecological standpoint, but more likely the reference is to the fact that America's inland waterways in 1976, for instance, carried 352 billion tons of cargo, not counting our overseas cargo. Yes, this mighty nation of the United States of America IS described in the Bible, and its destiny is foretold. This country will be severely hurt by a nuclear "battle by fire," but it will survive its ordeal and will continue as a nation until the end of time!

## WHEN WILL THIS HAPPEN?

The question that comes to us now is, When will this happen? What are the signs of the times? And how long do we have before the fury of World War III is unleashed?

As to the sinfulness of America, the time is ripe. Wickedness is rampant in our land, and the judgment of God is before us. His judgment could come at any time. Perhaps today. As to the affluence of America, we are the most highly developed and prosperous nation on the face of the earth. The time could be NOW. You might say, however, that we are not yet ready for such an attack. But we are preparing for one as rapidly as possible.

On September 10, 1982, President Ronald Reagan signed the current defence budget of almost $178 billion. This is to operate our armed forces and to develop and produce vast weaponry for just one year. On August 15, 1982, Los Angeles Times reported from Washington that the Pentagon last week, on the orders of the Reagan Administration, completed a strategic master plan to give the United States the capability of *winning* a protracted *nuclear war with the Soviet Union.*

How striking it is that our publicized enemy is the same one that the Bible proclaimed 2,500 years ago! Yes, Sirs, THE BIBLE IS RELIABLE.

What else will determine the time element? Three great factors are involved besides that of military preparedness. (We *must* prepare quickly, for every news release as well as every prophecy indicates that the Soviet Union and the Arab states will initiate a great attack against Israel, and they already are bristling with armament of all types.) The other three factors are:

1) The near proximity of the entry on the world scene of the "king" of the tribulation era—THE ANTICHRIST.

2) The Middle East buildup for the showdown fight with Israel over the land of Israel and its capital city, Jerusalem.

3) The spiritual event known as the rapture of the church, followed immediately by the unveiling of Lucifer's false church system referred to in Revelation 17 of the Bible as "BABYLON THE GREAT, MOTHER OF HARLOTS AND ABOMINATIONS OF THE EARTH." This false church system is portrayed in biblical allegory as being a woman of abominations riding on a scarlet-colored beast: a beast having ten horns. The Antichrist Beast of the Tribulation Period is to be a man, a military leader of a prophesied 10-nation revived Roman empire. The 10-nation Common Market of today is almost universally recognized as being the beginning of that revived Roman empire.

## THE NEW AGE MOVEMENT

The false church system that is to come on the world scene at the same time as the Antichrist king is to be Luciferian in doctrine, anti-Christian and anti-Semitic in attitude and intolerant in practice.

Revelation 17:6 states, "And I saw the woman drunken with the blood of the saints, and with the blood of the martyrs of Jesus."

The religion of abomination is in existance today and is epitomized in the NEW AGE MOVEMENT. It proclaims in "THE PLAN" thereof that all Christians, Jews and Moslems who will not participate in Luciferian initiation *must be put to death.* As H.G. Wells wrote in his book *The Open Conspiracy,* "We can't leave any of it," referring to the Christian church.

Advocating the Luciferian initiation, David Spangler, co-director of Findhorn Foundation in Scotland and reportedly one of the top leaders of the New Age Movement, wrote in his book *Reflections on the Christ,* "The light of the inner man, LUCIFER, works within wholeness as we move into the new age...Lucifer comes to give us this final gift of wholeness." Spangler also stated that all people *"had* to take it" if they wished to enter the New Age.

Yes, "the mark of the beast" will be required at its appointed time. All this is part of THE PLAN of the New Age Movement as it prepares NOW to introduce the world to its occult Aquarian Age.

The text book of the New Age Movement is *The Aquarian Gospel of Jesus Christ,* by Levi. It is an abominable adulteration of Bible texts that weaves their Luciferian doctrines into the life story of Jesus, saying He went to Egypt to receive instruction therein. Implying that Lucifer is the Light, chapter 8. verse 21 states, "The only devil from which man must be redeemed is self, the lower self. If man would find his devil he must look within; his name is self.

"If man would find his saviour he must look within; and when the demon self has been dethroned the saviour, Love, will be exalted to the throne of power."

In David Spangler's *Reflections of the Christ*, it is written: "The light of the inner man, LUCIFER, works within wholeness as we move into a new age...Lucifer comes to give us this final gift of wholeness."

To enforce its acceptance, the New Age Movement has established many para-military groups and organizations. Ananda Marga Yoga Society, for instance, is worldwide. A news report from San Jose, California, August 15, 1982, states: "A worldwide sect that runs yoga and meditation classes throughout the United States is under investigation by the FBI to determine if it is a foreign-based terrorist organization. In the 27 years since its founding, the cult has left a trail of blood around the world. Ananda Marga's guru, who spent seven years in an Indian jail on murder charges, predicts the cult will rule the world. It now claims a worldwide following of 3 million members in 30 countries."

## NEO-NAZIS AND GUARDIAN ANGELS

I also have found the Neo-Nazi organizations are on the rise, not only in West Germany, but also in the U.S.A. One faction, the Aryan Brothers, now reportedly is functioning throughout all the federal prisons, judging and punishing whom they will.

More openly, the very aggressive Guardian Angels have spread across this nation. Purporting to help the police, groups are patrolling the streets in many cities of the U.S. and Canada. They soon expect to exceed 100,000 in number. I offer this warning: Beware of them, for their training is reportedly similar to that of Hitler's Brown Shirts and it is said they are being positioned for the purpose of furthering the cause of the New Age Movement by slaying Christians and Jews when they get the signal from the Hierarchy. That signal may come sooner than you think! According the THE PLAN of the New Age Movement, they reportedly have a timetable whereby they hope to have their domination complete *by the summer solstice of 1983!*

## THE HINDERING FACTOR—THE CHURCH

But there is a hindering factor today—the presence of millions of God's people who constitute the believing Church.

Jesus said, "I will build my church, and the gates of hell shall not prevail against it." While the Born Again people, the true believers in Jesus, remain on this earth, Satan's forces are held in check. They are hindered from taking over the societies and governments of this world. But just as surely as the sun sets in the west, the time has almost arrived when the believers, the true church, will be "taken out of the way" as recorded in 2 Thessalonians. Verses 8 to 10 read:

"And *then* shall the Wicked One be revealed...Even him, whose coming is after the working of Satan with all power and signs and lying wonders, and with all deceivableness of unrighteousness in them that perish: because they received not the love of the truth (i.e., faith in Jesus) that they might be saved."

## TRIBULATION IS COMING

Great turmoil and destruction is coming. It will be a time of judgment and of great tribulation. Jesus predicted it in His day. He said in Matthew 24:21, "For then shall be great tribulation, such as was not since the beginning of the world to this time, no, nor ever shall be."

That time of great distress is not for the church, however. It is a time of trial and of circumstances so severe that men's hearts will fail them for fear. When the true Christians are removed from the earth "in the twinkling of an eye," as prophesied in the Bible, the anarchists and the rebellious ones will take over. The false church will persecute and kill any who try to carry on Christian or Jewish tradition. It will be a time of tremendous persecution!

What I am reporting here is the startling fact that such a ruthless form of religion already is present in the world, and it is busily engaged in enlarging and coordinating the many cults and occult groups into a worldwide unity of endeavor.

Mrs. Constance Cumby, an attorney from Detroit, has done some exhaustive research on the New Age Movement. She says they are following H.G. Wells' *Blueprint for a World Revolution* as recorded in his book entitled *The Open Conspiracy*. It is known as THE PLAN and is being carried out by Masters called "The Hierarchy." Alice Bailey was one ringleader of it and reportedly wrote the basic plan for the United Nations, describing it as a step toward the New World Order. Much detail is in Alice Bailey's book *The Externalization of the Hierarchy*, which is one that I have used in this research.

Why am I speaking of these things today? Because THE PLAN is almost ready for its final action. It very evidently will be the functioning basis for Satanic takeover of religion, social orders and governments in the soon-coming Tribulation Period. Thousands of organizations in many countries are involved. Tara Centers in New York and London and the Lucis (formerly Lucifer) Trust of London, New York and Geneva are two of the largest base organizations evident, but there are many more, of which the Illuminati was apparently only a small portion. One-Worlders of any order, from UNESCO to the Bilderbergers, all are part and portion of the vast New Age Movement. You cannot stop it any more than you could keep the sun from coming up in the morning. It has developed over the centuries and now is ready to assert itself—as soon as the hindering force is removed. I am not speaking of the restraining power of the United States Government, NATO or any other political force. I speak of the restraining power of the Spirit of God functioning in the church: the living church consisting of all true believers in Jesus, regardless of affiliation or fellowship. Without offense to any, let me explain what Bible-believing Christians have in common—what they believe.

God so loved the world that He gave his only begotten Son, Jesus, that WHOSOVER BELIEVES in Him should not perish, but have everlasting life. Jesus died on the cruel Roman tree on Calvary, outside the walls of Jerusalem. He bore our sins and became a curse for us. He became our substitute. He died in our place, SUFFERING FOR OUR SINS.

It is written in Isaiah 53, "All we like sheep have gone astray, we have turned *every one* to his own way; and the Lord hath laid on Him the iniquity of us all...He was cut off from the land of the living; for the transgression of my people was He stricken...Thou hast made Him an offering for sin." It is for EVERY ONE, for each individual who believes.

John, a disciple of Jesus, wrote in John 1:11 and 12, "He came unto His own and His own received Him not, but as many as received Him, to them gave He the power to become the sons of God, even to them that believe on His Name."

Again it is written, "WHOSOEVER shall call on the Name of the Lord shall be saved." The Way of salvation is by faith in Jesus as Savior, as Messiah and Lord. Jesus said, "You believe in God, believe also in Me...I go to prepare a place for you, and if I go and prepare a place for you, I will come again and receive you unto Myself, that where I am, there you may be also."

Yes, Jesus is coming again, and all prophecy indicates it will be in our lifetime. More importantly, it will be *soon.*

I Thessalonians 4:13-18 reads, "Sorrow not, even as others who have no hope. For if we believe that Jesus died and rose again, even so them also which sleep in Jesus will God bring with Him.

"For this we say unto you by the word of the Lord, that we which are alive and remain unto the coming of the Lord shall not precede them which have passed away. For the Lord Himself shall descend from heaven with a shout, with the voice of the archangel, and with the trump of God: and the dead in Christ shall rise first. Then we which are alive and remain (at that moment) shall be caught up together with them in the clouds to meet the Lord in the air: and so shall we forever be with the Lord.

"Wherefore comfort one another with these words."

It is, indeed, a comfort to the true Christians to know that "God hath not appointed us to wrath, but to obtain salvation by our Lord Jesus Christ."

The next great event to take place in God's calendar, Sirs, is going to be the sounding of the trumpet of God and the calling of all truly born-again Christians out of this wicked world. Seven years of great trouble, called the Tribulation Period, is about to start. When the believers in Jesus are taken out of this world "in the twinkling of an eye," as written in I Corinthians 15, the panorama of end-time events, prophesied in many places in the Bible, will start to be fulfilled.

You, President Reagan (for I understand that you are a believing Christian), many members of the Cabinet and of Congress and also a great many leaders in the Pentagon will suddenly be translated from earth to heaven. Each had made his personal decision to trust in Jesus as Messiah-Savior and was taken to be with Him in Glory.

Those who remain will be in shock. They didn't think that such an event could happen. But it did. Now what?

## THE ORDER OF EVENTS TO COME

Christians from all countries will have disappeared. Many police officers and public servants will be gone. Most had applied for their positions because they cared for people. They were true Christians with love in their hearts. Now they are gone. Many moral people, however sincere, will still remain on earth, for they did not put their trust in Jesus for the forgiveness of sin. They could not be taken without faith in the Lord.

The unbelieving, the crooked and perverse, the hypocrites and naves will remain. What kind of order will they be able to bring out of all the confusion? They will have a little success, but not as it is today. There will be looting of the homes and businesses of those who were believing Christians and were taken from this world into God's perfect Heaven. Anarchy and revolution will follow. The deluded Guardian Angel organization and other cultists and the occult will start to take over.

Internationally, there will be activity. Not many, if any, of Russia's leaders will be taken, for their religion is atheism. And since their avowed aim is world domination, they will be anxious to take advantage of the turmoil: to strike before those remaining in the United States and Western Europe can reorganize.

In the Muslim nations as well, not believing in Jesus as Savior, most of their leaders still will be in power. The great war over Jerusalem will take place—the war we commonly call World War III. I described the nations to be involved in that war in the early portion of this message.

The eleventh nation, probably Spain, will join the European Community, the Common Market. The prophesied military leader thereof will offer to lead Western Europe in its fight against the Soviet Union. Also, he will guarantee Israel's security in fulfillment of specific Bible prophecy. Watch for him to change nations in the 10-nation Common Market, uprooting three nations and replacing them with three others, as recorded in Daniel 7:8, 24 and 25. It will be a sudden change, but will be accomplished to strengthen the military position of Western Europe.

Denmark, Ireland and Greece most likely will be dropped from the European Community. Greenland, which belongs to Denmark, already has voted by referendum to leave the Common Market. This was done February 24, 1982. And Denmark, itself, never was a part of the old Roman empire.

Greece was a part of the Roman empire, but Andreas Papandreou was elected Prime Minister last year on the platform of seceding from the European Community and from NATO. He has not yet done so, but has greatly befriended Yasser Arafat of the PLO, Israel's avowed enemy. I have talked to the editor of the *Athens News* personally and I find at Greece is extremely pro-Arab and anti-Israel. It would not agree to defend Israel.

Since Western Europe, under the leadership of the Antichrist king of the Tribulation, is destined to fight *for* Israel, defending it from the Soviets and Arabs, Greece most likely will be dropped.

Ireland, not a member of NATO and having many communists in its population, probably will be the other nation to be eliminated.

On the other side of the coin, Spain and Portugal move together historically; and a third country, Austria, is vital to Western Europe, serving as a buffer between Eastern Europe and Italy. Also, all three of these nations already have applied for membership in the Common Market.

It is thus that we find that three nations of today are ready to join the 10-nation Common Market and three nations are likely to be dropped—*just as prophesied in the Bible.* And Daniel 7 states that it will be the end-time king (the Antichrist) who will "uproot three kings." He's the one who will do it. All seems ready for his appearance!

It is not unadvisedly nor glibly that I say to you, BE READY. The "rapture of the church" will take place and the tribulation era will begin. THIS COULD BE THE YEAR, for all groups and nations now are aligning as prophesied.

## RESULTS OF THE NUCLEAR WAR

Here is the outline of events that are sure to happen in the United States, in Western Europe, Israel, the Arab countries and the Soviet Union. Bible prophecy is very specific about the outcome of World War III.

A study of the prophecies of Ezekiel, Daniel, Isaiah and Joel in the Bible and of the prophecies of Jesus in the Gospels and in the Revelation reveals that the Arab nations, together with the Soviet and Warsaw Pact armies, will start a massive attack against Israel. Such an attack will bring the powers of Western Europe and the United States of America to the defense of Israel. A great "battle by fire" is described by Isaiah and Joel and in the Revelation. Isaiah wrote, "Their faces shall be as flames."

Joel wrote in his second chapter, "...A great people and a strong: there hath not ever been the like, neither shall be after it, even to the years of many generations. A *fire* burneth before them, and behind them a *flame* burneth: the land is as the garden of Eden before them, and behind them a desolate wilderness; yea, and nothing shall escape them."

What a picture of nuclear warfare! As the garden of Eden before them, and behind them a desolate wilderness. The fireball flash devours and the fire-storm flame follows to destroy the balance. And this prophecy was written in the chariot-racing days-eight hundred years before Jesus walked on this earth. Yes, Bible prophecy is astounding in its description, in its detail and in its accuracy.

Ezekiel 39 says of the Soviet Union, "I will *send a fire* on the land of Magog (industrial Russia). Documents I have on hand indicate that the U.S.A. now has over 25,000 nuclear warheads, and most of them are aimed at Russia. That's enough to make a cinder out of all the cities of the Soviet Union.

Ezekiel 39:8 says, "Behold, it is come and it is done, saith the Lord God: this is *the day* whereof I have spoken."

When the nuclear exchange starts (in which the U.S. will be greatly damaged but not destroyed), it will happen in one horrendous day. It will be "kill or be killed." Every missile will go.

The Soviet Union has almost as many warheads aimed at us. Many will get through our meager defense. Bible prophecy will be fulfilled and this nation will be greatly "pruned" and "cut," but it will survive.

## CRISIS RELOCATION AND SURVIVAL

Realizing that this is a very real situation and that extensive preparations now are being made by our Office of Civil Defense, the Defense Department's Civil Preparedness Agency and many other governmental divisions, and seeing that Congress just passed a $178 billion defense budget for fiscal 1983, what does this preponderance of evidence mean to us as individuals? Where do we go from here?

According to Crisis Relocation Planning, the people of the U.S.A. should leave, or be ready to vacate, all cities near military installations, all technical and industrial areas that would be sure targets and all cities of more than 50,000 population. MAD—Massive Assured Destruction—still is the avowed plan of both the U.S.S.R. and the U.S.A. It calls for the destruction of all major cities.

Some provisions already have been made. For instance, the Postal Service will issue postage-free "emergency change-of-address cards" and the Department of Agriculture now has a food rationing system to distribute, among other things, six eggs and four pounds of cereal to every surviving American each week, according to an article in TIME Magazine, March 29, 1982. Also, the President has budgeted $252 million for civil defense for 1983. That is just a start!

April 12, 1982, U.S. News and World Report: "The Soviet Union has spent billions to create what may be the world's most extensive civil defense system. Behind the scenes, the Soviets have done far more than the U.S. to protect their leadership, their essential work force and their population." (The article goes on to explain much detail of their survival preparations.)

April 12, 1982, U.S. News and World Report: "Amid rising controversy over President Reagan's nuclear-arms policy, a White House plan for a vast new civil defense program has ignited a political firestorm. The plan spelled out in March calls, in case of nuclear showdown with the Soviet Union, for evacuating to the countryside the 145 million Americans living in 400 high-risk areas in big cities and near vital military bases.

"Experts predict that an all-out nuclear attack today pobably would kill some 139 million of the nation's population of 231 million. Proponents claim the new plan would cut the death toll to about 46 million.

"The new civil-defense scheme differs significantly from

those put forward in the 1950's and 1960's, largely because of the enormous rise in the number of nuclear weapons now aimed at the U.S. Now the assumption is that 400 targets—all the U.S. cities of more than 50,000 population, the bomber and nuclear-submarine bases, the missile silos and other military and industrial sites—might be hit almost simultaneously. The number of Americans living or working in those high-risk areas totals 145 million, and for them there would be no place to hide.

"The new plan is to move them out into the countryside to host areas where they would be relatively safe from blast, heat and the initial burst of nuclear radition. They would require protection—perhaps for weeks. When people from the cities reached the countryside, many would be put to work. Some would operate kitchens for mass feeding. Others would be handed shovels and told to stack dirt around shelters for protection against radition from nuclear fallout.

"Evacuees would be housed in schools, churches and other public buildings, not in private homes. Engineering students hired during the summer already have checked out 975,000 of the 1.6 million shelters needed."

On and on go the reports. Yes, *the United States is preparing for survival.* The war almost is upon us. Almost every paper and news magazine of today has military or civil defense information and articles about the aggression of the Soviet Union.

The Bible has given the prophecies and now the news media confirms them. The nations listed in the Bible as being in confrontation "at the time of the end" now are poised and their armaments are "at the ready." Time is running out.

Before I give some special suggestions, let me tell you of two books I have written that will give far more detail than I can include in this message. *WORLD WAR III AND THE DESTINY*

*Beware America*

*OF AMERICA* is extremely popular and the most comprehensive book on Bible prophecies available anywhere. It has 773 Bible references explained in detail and fully indexed. These are clarified by history, geography and scientific data and are verified by over 100 documented news reports, plus many pictures and maps. If you are concerned for the U.S.A. and its people, you need this extensive report of America's role in today's world. And it could save your life! This 360-page can be ordered from TODAY IN BIBLE PROPHECY, P.O. BOX 5700, HUNTINGTON BEACH, CA 92615. The price of the hardbound library edition is $7.95, or it is available in a quality paperback for just $5.95.

A smaller sequel to this book is *THOSE WHO REMAIN*. It has 104 pages of vital information pertaining to developments in the U.S.A., Europe and the Middle East. Prophecies of coming events are explained and suggestions are given for survival during and after the nuclear war. It tells what to expect and what to do about it. Retail price of this book is just $2.95.

Current events are documented, compared with Bible prophecy and supplied in graphic form in *BIBLE PROPHECY NEWS*. This booklet is sent to over 50,000 homes in the U.S. and Canada every three months, being provided on a contribution basis. Send a tax-deductible contribution of any amount to TODAY IN BIBLE PROPHECY, INC., P.O. BOX 5700, HUNTINGTON BEACH, CA 92615 and ask for *BIBLE PROPHECY NEWS*. You will be amazed at its content, for I document news from around the world. This booklet also contains my national TV schedule (on satellite four times a week) and a listing of many of my books and cassettes now available.

### SOME HELPFUL SUGGESTIONS

In order to delay the nuclear exchange as long as possible, our leaders in Congress should restrict even further the export of our technology and our industrial equipment to the Soviet Union or any countries that are likely to transfer that material or information to the U.S.S.R. We *must* desist from feeding the monster that plots our destruction!

We must become as energy independent as possible, utilizing solar, thermal, wind, gas, nuclear and every other form of energy such as gasohol and methane. We must find and develop as much oil as possible. And we must reduce the outlandish waste of our natural resources by recycling and reproducing at every opportunity.

After the nuclear exchange, safe water will be a prime factor. Research and development of underground water storage would be a prime concern, and it needs to be done immediately. Warn all people: After any nuclear attack, do not drink from open streams! Any open water will be poisoned by radioactive fallout. Do not even drink milk, for the cows will be contaminated by direct fallout or by drinking from water sources that are contaminated. Use bottled water or canned or bottled drinks. Boiling the water will not eliminate radiation. If there is any question about the water, leave it alone. Remember that the Bible states in Revelation 8:11, *"Many men will die of the waters, because they are made bitter* (radioactive)."

If you don't know the Lord as your Savior today, get a Bible and read it, for its prophecies and messages have the full plan for your redemption and salvation.

Beware of any phase of the New Age Movement or any followers of Lucifer, the Satan of the Bible. Believing in reincarnation (which is absolutely a false doctrine), they will believe they are doing you a favor by "sending you to another dimension where you will be happier." That is their terminology and excuse for genocide—the murder of all who do not follow their ideas and THE PLAN. They will eliminate you from their Age of Aquarius, the New Age.

In Revelation, chapter 7, we are told there will be 144,000 JEWISH evangelists who will have the Father's Name sealed in their foreheads. They will be the true witnesses of God after the believers in Jesus have been "caught up" to meet the Lord in the clouds at "the rapture of the church." Believe these chosen Jewish messengers—if they have the prophesied seal of God's Name in their foreheads. This will be a literal seal, or mark: not a symbolic spirituality as some people say, and it will serve to separate the true from the false.

Also, two prophets of God will appear as teachers (witnesses) in Jerusalem. They will have the true message about the return of the Messiah to establish His reign of Peace on Earth. Jesus (Yeshua) will come as the Messiah almost exactly seven years after the disappearance of the Christians at "the rapture of the church." At this time He will establish His rule as King of Salem—King of Peace—and there will be perfect peace on earth for 1,000 years. At His coming, He will destroy Lucifer and the works of Satan at the Battle of Armageddon. *Then* there will be a true millenium of peace on earth, good will to all men. Yes, VICTORY IS COMING!

## FIRST, "THE MARK OF THE BEAST"

Before the great Victory of the Messiah, there is to be a seven-year period of suffering referred to by Daniel as "the time of Jacob's trouble" and called by the Christians the Tribulation Period. In the middle of that time, a decree will be issued that all people must receive a special mark or number in their forehead or their right hand. It will be the number of the Antichrist, number 666. No one will be allowed to buy or sell anything without this number or mark. It is called "the mark of the beast" in Bible terminology and will only be given to those who signify their worship of the Antichrist king, the Beast, Lucifer incarnate, for by the middle of the seven-year period Lucifer will have taken possession of the body of his puppet king. Any who receive this mark or number will identify with Lucifer, but instead of receiving initation to an Aquarian life in a New Age, they will be sealing their doom because Lucifer and all his followers will be totally defeated by the King of kings, the Messiah, when He comes in power at the end of the Tribulation Period.

God's warning about receiving "the mark of the beast" is recorded in Revelation 14:9-11, quote, "If any man worship the beast and his image, and receive his mark in his forehead, or in his hand, the same shall drink of the wrath of God, which is poured out without mixture into the cup of His indignation; and he shall be tormented with fire and brimstone in the presence of the holy angels, and in the presence of the Lamb; and the smoke of their torment ascendeth up for ever and ever. and they have no rest day or night, who worship the beast and his image, and whosoever receiveth the mark of his name."

Do not allow this mark to be placed on your body, or, when Jesus comes in power at the end of the seven years, you will be cast into tormenting flame for ever. The number *666 will represent Lucifer, whose destiny is eternal torment in flames for all the evil he has done. Refuse his mark at all cost. It will be far better to be a martyr for Jesus and go to be with Him in the glories of heaven than to buy only three and one-half years of evil life on earth and then spend the rest of eternity with Lucifer and his demons in the lake of fire. DO NOT WORSHIP LUCIFER. WORSHIP GOD.

---

*Do not be afraid of the present usage of 666, for today it is only a convenient computer number. Realize however, that the technology for worldwide use of it as a worship sign already is evident. But do *not* allow it to be put on your forehead or hand, signifying obedience or worship.

## MY ADMONITION

My admonition to all who hear or read this message is, put your faith in God and believe the promises of His book, the Bible. Its message is true. For God so loved the world that He gave His only begotten Son, that whosoever believes in Him should not perish, but have everlasting life. For God sent not His Son into the world to condemn the world, but that the world through Him might be saved.

Believe in the Lord Jesus (Yeshua) as Redeemer, as Messiah, as your Savior. He loves you so much that He died for you on a cruel Roman cross, paying the penalty for your sins (and mine). He wants you to be with Him in the beauties of heaven, not with Lucifer in a Devil's hell. Trust in Jesus as your Redeemer and Savior today. Let Him forgive all your sins and shame. It is written, "The wages of sin is death, but *the gift of God is eternal life through Jesus Christ our Lord*" (Romans 6:23). Let Him give YOU the Life that is eternal.

Let me help you. Please repeat this simple prayer: "O Lord God in heaven, I have done wrong and I confess it to you now. I come to you to ask forgiveness for all my sins. I believe that Jesus sacrificed His perfect life to save all who would put their trust in Him, and I accept Him as my perfect Savior right now. I believe that His blood has washed away all my sin and made me whole. Now, by faith, I am a child of God. Thank you, Lord, for saving my soul. I will do my best to tell others of your wonderful salvation... Amen.

It is written, "Whosoever shall call on the name of the Lord shall be saved." When you said the prayer, you were calling on the name of the Lord Jesus. You trusted in His word and He is faithful to His word. He has given you eternal life and your faith in Him made you a citizen of heaven. I'll meet you there when this life is over.

In the meantime, you need to grow as a Christian. Faith comes by hearing, and hearing by the word of God. Read the Bible every day. Talk to God in prayer. Tell others about Jesus and His love.

Proverbs 3:5 and 6 reads, "Trust in the Lord with all your heart and lean not on your own understanding. In all your ways acknowledge Him, and He will direct your paths."

## SUMMARY

This is the message I sent to the President of the United States of America, to the Cabinet members and to the members of Congress.

Although judgment is coming to this land, America will endure its time of trial and will continue as a nation. If God be for us, who can be against us? Blessed is the nation whose God is the Lord. America will learn its lesson in its fullness when Jesus comes as King of kings at the end of the seven-year era of tribulation. Then this nation will serve the Lord and live in peace.

You do not have to go through that tribulation, however. All who trust in Jesus as Lord and Savior at the present time will be "caught up" in the clouds to meet the Lord in the air when He comes for us "in the twinkling of an eye" at the time of the rapture of the church. That event, my friends, is to take place BEFORE the war described as World War III. Since the precise nations listed in the Bible as being involved in that war are now lining up in their respective positions, either against Israel or in defense of Israel, and since the revived Roman empire is seen in the prophesied 10-nation coalition of the Common Market of today, we KNOW that "the time of the end" is almost here. Everything seems ready for the king of the Tribulation Period, the false king, the Antichrist, to come to the scene. Therefore, the time for Jesus to come in the clouds for His church, to take the hindering factor out of the way, is very, very near.

No man knows the day or the hour, but Jesus gave us "the signs of the times" and told us to "watch." I have been watching and documenting the news events for many years, and now the time has come to warn all people and to alert them to the fact that JESUS IS COMING SOON.

Satan's Antichrist will have a short seven years of dominion on earth during which time there will be severe tribulation and judgment. Then at last Jesus will come to earth, standing in that day on the Mount of Olives as Yeshua ha Mashiah, King of kings. Fighting for His people, Israel, He will defeat and destroy the works of the Devil, Lucifer-Satan, and will establish PEACE ON EARTH, GOODWILL TO MEN.

It is written in I Corinthians 15:57: *"Now thanks be to God that giveth us the victory through our Lord Jesus Christ."*

God bless you and keep you in the hollow of His hand. Amen.

## CURRENT PROPHECY INFORMATION

*Today in Bible Prophecy* is the television program produced by Dr. Charles Taylor. This weekly program updates the news and compares it with the prophecies of the Bible, revealing many prophecy fulfillments. It is carried on many stations across the U.S. and is broadcast to hundreds of cable and transponder stations by satellite.

Check the TV Guide for listings in your area or see the TV Log in *Bible Prophecy News.*

*Bible Prophecy News* is a periodical published regularly by Today in Bible Prophecy, Inc. to provide up-to-date news related to Bible prophecy as researched and documented by Dr. Charles Taylor. Over 50,000 are distributed worldwide. *Bible Prophecy News* is provided on a contribution basis. All gifts in the U.S.A. or Canada are income tax deductible.

To receive *Bible Prophecy News*, send a contribution to

Today in Bible Prophecy, Inc.
P.O. Box 5700
Huntington Beach, CA 92615
or
Today In Bible Prophecy
104 Consumers Drive
Whitby, ON L1N 5T3

## BOOKS BY DR. CHARLES R. TAYLOR

WORLD WAR III AND THE DESTINY OF AMERICA
 The most extensively documented book ever printed pertaining to specific Bible prophecy fulfillments in this generation. 773 Bible references are coordinated with over 100 news articles giving amazing information. Illustrated with maps and pictures. 390 pages: Paperback $5.95. Hardback $7.95.

GET ALL EXCITED—JESUS IS COMING SOON
 An exciting book giving specific information about end-time events. It deals specifically with prophecies related to the land of Israel and with *the rapture of the church*. 108 pages, illustrated: Paperback $2.95.

THOSE WHO REMAIN
 This book, published in 1980, gives Bible prophecies about the Tribulation Period and suggestions for survival during that time. It contains many U.S. government plans for crisis relocation and other contingencies for survival during and after nuclear conflagration. Also, it gives Bible prophecy information and God's plan for spiritual salvation during the Tribulation Period. A challenging book. 103 pages: Paperback $2.95.

## PRETRIBULATION RAPTURE AND THE BIBLE

A book containing almost 100 Bible references, including salvation portions. It verifies that the Church will not go through any portion of the Tribulation Period. Very helpful in explaining this fact to those who doubt. 40 pages: Paperback $1.50.

## 666 IS HERE (Tract)

An 8-page fold-out tract with illustrations showing that the UPC code could be used as "the mark of the beast" and that 666 could serve as "the number of his name" as prophesied in the Bible. The mark or number will not be required until the middle of the Tribulation, but *the technology for it is here today.* Has Bible warnings, startling scientific facts and gospel impact. 50 for $5.00 or 100 for $7.50, (Also in Spanish—same price).

## **CASSETTES BY DR. CHARLES R. TAYLOR**

## COUNTDOWN TO THE RAPTURE

A one hour message giving details of prophecies being fulfilled and yet to be fulfilled. It reveals that almost nothing remains to be done and that the *rapture* is very near. A helpful soul-winning item: $4.95.

## REVELATION TAUGHT IN CHRONOLOGICAL ORDER

A complete study of Revelation coordinated with the Old Testament prophecies and the teachings of Christ as taught in chronological arrangement on 215 radio broadcasts. Most complete comprehensive study available anywhere. First 16 cassette album: $69.95; Second 16 cassette album: $69.95; Third 12 cassette album: $49.95. Individual cassettes: $4.95.

## BEWARE AMERICA

This book in cassette form. $5.95.

How to Order Books or Cassettes

Send cash, check or money order to
TODAY IN BIBLE PROPHECY, INC.
P.O. Box 5700
Huntington Beach, CA 92615

20% discount for 12 or more items to one address
REGULAR TRADE DISCOUNT FOR ALL BOOKSTORES

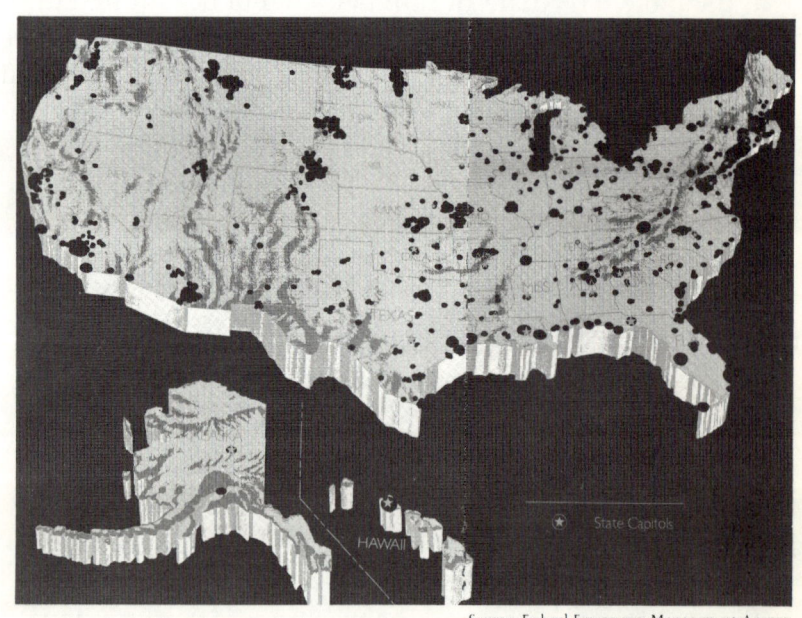

Source: Federal Emergency Management Agency

**WHERE THE BOMBS WOULD FALL**